It's the twins. The Bratt twins, Fred and Wilf, skid into the soft sand at the end of the pond.

'Let's spit in the pond,' said Fred. 'Let's swat all the bugs and step on the slugs,' said Wilf.

'Let's flip the log and drop it in,' said Fred. 'Let's dam it up. Let's rip up lots of grass and clog the pond up,' said Wilf.

'Yes!' the twins yell, grin, and slap hands.

Fran skipped up to the end of the pond.
'Oh, no. The Bratt twins are pests,' she said. Fran hid.

'If the pond is a mess, it will silt up and the frogs can't swim. I must stop the twins. But can I?'

'Can I get Fred to slip in the wet mud?'

'Can I set a trap to stop Wilf?'

'Can I slap Wilf's legs?'

'Can I trip Fred up?'

'No, I am not as big as the twins. And Fred and Wilf tend to hit a lot.'

Next, the twins snap some twigs and stab at the frogs. The frogs jump up and hop off.
Fran gets cross. 'Stop it!' she yells.

The twins stop. 'Run, get the kid!' Fred yells to Wilf.

Fran sped off. 'I must not trip up.' Fran felt stiff stems of grass stab her legs, but still she ran on. 'I must not trip up.'

Slip! Fran fell. Grit dug into the skin on her hands. She felt a hand grab the top of her dress and lift her up. Was it Wilf . . . or Fred?

No! It was Miss Scott. 'Fran! Did you trip up?'
'Miss Scott,' said Fran, 'the Bratt twins will clog up the pond and kill the bugs and slugs and . . . I must stop the twins!'

'But you must ask for help, Fran. I'm glad to help. I'll get the twins to stop,' Miss Scott said.

Wilf ran up. Slam! He felt the red stuff from Miss Scott's tins drip on his skin. Fred ran up. Snap! He trod on Miss Scott's steps. He felt a hand drag him up. 'Get up,' said Miss Scott. She was cross.

'Fix it. Get in the pond. Get the log, the twigs and the grass and put it all on the bank.'

Miss Scott and Fran sat on the soft moss. The twins did the job and left. Plop! Plop! The frogs swam in the pond.

'Yes!' said Miss Scott and Fran.